aliza

forgetting

you

never mistake me
for a second choice

aliza grace

i love rain
i love the way rain sounds at night on a tin roof
when the rest of the town is asleep
im left awake daydreaming about you
listening to the rain escape the sky
quite like tears escaped my eyes
the day we broke up

im just a poet
writing about love
in a world where
i love you
never means
i wont leave you

i did it
i deleted the pictures
the ones at the beginning of my camera roll
the photos i looked at every night when you crossed
my mind
the funny thing is that was never the hardest thing to
do
the hardest thing to do was realizing that the boy in
them who i loved for so long
changed

aliza grace

you stapled my mouth shut
then screamed at me to speak

aliza grace

it only hurts this bad
because you really loved them

i woke up crying
the other night
because you wasnt
in bed with me

i miss picking up the trash in front of the can
because you could never throw it in
i miss shutting the shower curtain
because you always left it open
i miss looking for the remote together
because you never put it in the same place as before
i miss making dinner for two
because you always told me how much you loved
my cooking

car rides arent the same
its not your favorite rock band on the radio anymore
now its phoebe bridgers and mitski

i wonder what you told them all
your family and friends
did you tell them how i
broke myself loving you
how i gave and gave
and still couldnt pour enough
to fill your cup
tell me did your mother
try to talk you out of it

aliza grace

i placed a polaroid of you

in the corner of every mirror

in the house we once shared

the house i wanted to start a family in

the house we had our first and last argument in

the house we broke up in

the house i cant go in anymore

.

i was always told good things never come easy
and i was so sure
you were my good thing
because nothing about our relationship was easy
yet we tried so hard to make it work

but it didnt

all the words
i have ever spoke to you

do they play over and over
in your head at night

do the memories of me visit
at the end of a long day
when your longing for comfort

can you still taste my kiss on your lips
and the sadness in my breath

have you gone through all the notions
of trying to call me to apologize

are you afraid of what i might say when i answer
how you know ill ask why you did it

if you were thinking of me
while you were laying beside of her

how did she
take your breathe away

you had me

for the longest time
i was at a loss of words
a loss of emotions
even after trying to
gather my words and emotions
there not here anymore

they left my body the day you cheated

i cant make you love me
but i can make you regret not loving me

why did all the lies
taste so sweet
coming from your lips

i mistook it for love

if you loved me
you would have never
said the things
you said to me

you said you loved me and only me
you said it was my feelings before yours
you said i meant the world to you
but you couldnt change
you wouldnt stop
so did i ever really mean
that much

aliza grace

the day you left
it was so sad
even the sky cried

aliza grace

did she
breathe life
in your dead soul

aliza grace

friends you said
but friends dont talk to each other
how you talked to her

friends you said
but you chose a friend over me
your girlfriend

i could taste the heartbreak
on your lips
the taste
was so
familiar

aliza grace

you dont know heartbreak
            until your significant other
                        looks you in the eyes
promising they didnt cheat
            when you know they did
                        you found the messages

aliza grace

my soul will always want you
my heart will never move on
my mind will always miss you

your voice
it sounds just like his

finding pieces of him in you

you are too full of life
to be half loved

aliza grace

if you want me
act like it

ignoring me
is the best way
to never hear from me
ever again

aliza grace

maturing is when
you realize silence
is better than arguing

overthinking
was
her
worst
enemy

aliza grace

its strange
how your not
here with me

i hate that youre happy
without me

aliza grace

i wish my touch
made me tremble
the way hers does

aliza grace

how heavy
does it make your heart
to watch your significant others eyes wander

aliza grace

some nights i wonder
if you ever look at the holes
in your walls and think about me

screaming
fighting
crying
laughing
smiling
living
giving
taking
talking
listening

our relationship

that feeling
i have felt it too
for far too long
that feeling is the one
burned in my bones
the feeling i cant forget
its a part of me now
just as its part of you

figuring out what he done

let yourself feel hurt
cry when you need to
find comfort in knowing
this wont last forever

aliza grace

i want to unmeet
a lot of people

stop seeing yourself
through the eyes
of someone
who never
saw you

sure i moved on
but i didnt really *move on*
i still look our pictures and cry
but i dont reach out

you call me pretty
but you look at other women

and i wonder why im not pretty enough
to keep your eyes on just me

aliza grace

what about her was so mesmerizing
was it the shape of her hips that made you forget me
or was it the curve of her body in the dark
was it the noises she made
that sounded nothing like me
did she know exactly what to do
without you telling her

tell me was it her
or was it just her
because she wasnt me

blue eyes
he said something about your blue eyes
how he couldnt see mine
how your eyes made him forget me

aliza grace

some days
i look in the mirror
and feel defeated

i stopped weighing myself
because the numbers feel defining

i wish you could feel
what you put me through
all the thoughts that ran through my mind

you really broke me
but you are fine

sorry
he said
as if he was actually sorry
as if a word could fit in every ounce of pity
he would need to get me to forgive him
as if he would be forgiven so soon

sorry
as in im sorry for destroying our relationship
as in im sorry for breaking your trust and your heart
as in im sorry for building wall so high no one else
will ever be allowed in
as in im sorry for giving you insecurities and trust
issues
as in im sorry for making you believe i was serious
about us and this relationship
as in im sorry for cheating on you

it wasnt any of that
it was just
sorry

you dont know pain
until you find something
on his phone
you wasnt suppose to find

he looked like
the sound rain on a tin roof makes

and when he left the thunder came

how to lose my attention:
liking other girls pictures

aliza grace

they asked me why i never left
as if it wasnt something i thought about constantly
as if staying didnt make me feel guilty

when you left
you took my voice with you

aliza grace

you tell me my body is perfect
while choosing to look at other girls

it doesnt feel like it

he said i was his everything
with porn in his browsing history
he told me my feelings mean the most
with porn in his browsing history
after i told him it hurt me

feeling like you will never be enough
to please your partner

one day i will leave
ill run so far away
and i wont look back

daydreaming

sometimes i wonder if you miss your past
and all the girls you left in it

aliza grace

i hope being without me
feels heavy and weighs on your heart
thats how i felt when i caught you looking at her

aliza grace

you forgot my birthday
you never asked my favorite color
i dont even think you really knew any small
detail about me or the things i enjoyed doing

but six months
was so long at that age i couldnt leave

aliza grace

i hate myself for allowing you back in
for giving you trust when you deserved none

i never got to accept your apology
because you never said sorry

dont let him win
get out of bed
put on that outfit he never let you wear out
listen to your feel good playlist

healing starts now

aliza grace

the problem
the real problem

is i would still choose you
after all the arguments and hate

i would choose you over
and over

again and again

aliza grace

try to forget me
go ahead and try

i promise you
it will hit hard when you least expect it

she could never love you
like i once did

and this will rip your heart
out of your chest

aliza grace

what made you remember her name
and forget mine

aliza grace

it was never meant to be
i didnt want to realize that

trying to forget you
was like trying to forget
the back of my hand
i see it everyday

a kiss fell from his lips
onto mine
as words i wished i would never hear
escaped
its over
the silence was so loud
he took me in his arms
while i gathered my thoughts
only to find there was not any
only to find myself in awe
after everything we went through
was tossed out and meaningless
our love disappeared with two words

my fingertips danced on your chest
i noticed a sparkle in your eye
one that was never there before
and my mood changed

a week before i found out you cheated

aliza grace

how do you live with knowing you crushed
the heart of a girl who thought so highly of you
the girl who protected your name
when every bitter thing they said about you was true

did he leave you forgetting what power you hold
you are woman
the portal between the spiritual realm and the
physical realm
you are intuitively and creatively driven
it is no coincidence that children and animals feel
safe with you
you are a unique form of walking art
a divine being that is emitting so much power
so selfless and giving
there is a reason society has tried for so long
to keep women down
the amount of power we all hold is astronomical
never forget who you are

aliza grace

instead of forcing such a strict dress code
we should demand to be treated like humans
men are never told that their legs arms or stomachs
are a problem
because they are treated like human beings
and not as sexual exploits

this is your sign
check his phone
go through his tik tok likes
insta saved
screen time
deleted apps
reddit
discord
twitter
youll look at him different

aliza grace

i spent nights washing your touch
from my skin
but morning comes
i wake up still thinking about you
still thinking about how you left without a care

aliza grace

for so long i thought love
looked like a tall dark haired man
and felt like a movie scene

love is so much more

its midnight i reach for my phone to text you
finding out you texted me first
come over
i wont lie i thought about it
all night
even now
but i didnt
i finally know my worth

you were the biggest red flag
red is my favorite color

aliza grace